Learn Hebrew Letters

The Aleph Bet Story

A Journey to the Tent
&

the Garden

Author & Illustrator

Kingdom Khai Books

Table of Contents:

Shalom/Welcome!

Welcome to the Aleph Bet Story Book!

Did you know,
all the Ancient Pictograph Hebrew letters
of the Hebrew Alephbet (Alphabet),
were picture symbols?

Each one carried it's own special meaning.

We've included a few short diagrams that show
the relationship between the letters,
their definitions, and their characters in the book.

Read, learn and enjoy the adventure :)

II

Diagram #1:

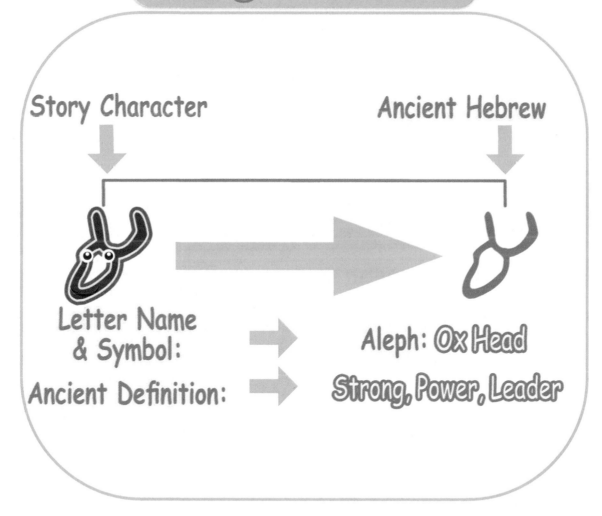

Story Character

Ancient Hebrew

Letter Name
& Symbol: ➡️ Aleph: Ox Head

Ancient Definition: ➡️ Strong, Power, Leader

III

Insight

With the understanding of the previous diagram, we can now think of today's Modern Hebrew letters as relatives to their earlier ancient ancestors.

Picture the Modern Aleph Bet letters as the Grandchildren of the Ancient Aleph Bet letters. Check out the next diagram:)

IV

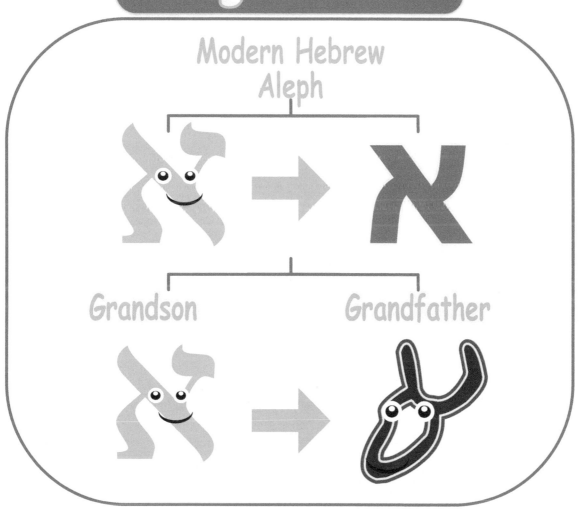

V

Story Time

"Below you will see the entire Hebrew Alphabet in both Ancient Hebrew and Modern Hebrew"

Ancient Hebrew

‎+ω⊕ⴸⴹⳑ⌐◎≢ⴶ᙭⥾᙭⊕ⵝ⵿ⲩⵕ⵿⊙ⴷ⊻

Modern Hebrew

אבגדהוזחטיכלמנסעפצקרשת

1

In a cozy little room with
a warm fireplace blazing,
Grandfather Aleph,
with his long white beard
And wise twinkling eyes,
sat in his favorite rocking chair.

In front of him
perched eagerly in his own chair,
was his grandson,
Modern Aleph, a lively and curious
young letter with a bright smile!

"Grandpa,
can you tell me
the story of the history of our family?",
Aleph said.

Grandpa replied, "Are you really ready,
it's a very special story?"

4

"Alright,
this is the story about our family,
The Hebrew Alephbet,
and the amazing meanings hidden within each of us!"

"Sit back and enjoy, it's going to be an adventure!"

6

Once upon a time there was,

†ω♙↳⌐⊙⧧⌐ᵐ⦉⨆⨄⊕Ⴕ⩱ΥΨ◌⌒◻⋎

And he was...

†ᘯꙄ𐤒ᒐ└☉≭ᘰᛖ⟨Ш⟩⌇◯ƟΗⵣⵗΨꝺ⋀𐤙

and he sees...

12

ༀⵡ⍟ꟼᛈᚳ⌐◉ꜚᕲ㎜⑩⤙⊕ℍⵉᛉꟺ◻ꭥ

"Oh no" then, he sees...

14

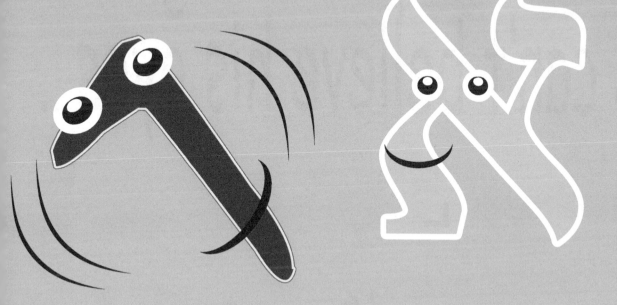

⟨symbols⟩

Mr. Ox keeps walking.
He can't believe his eyes...

16

He sees...

18

†ⲱ𝕬ⲣ⅂◉⧖ꞁ𝓂⟮⨄⟯⏌𐊀⊕𐊅⅄Ψ𐊠ᴧ⊡ᴪ

And above the door it said...

20

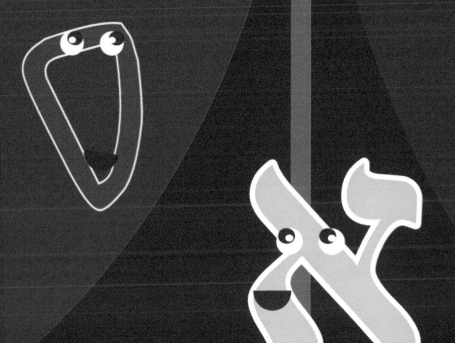

⊕↑ᗯᏈ⏁ᒪ◉₮ᕲᗰ⟮⫴⟯〜⊕╫≡Ƴ�◌

But too afraid to enter,
he went to the back...

22

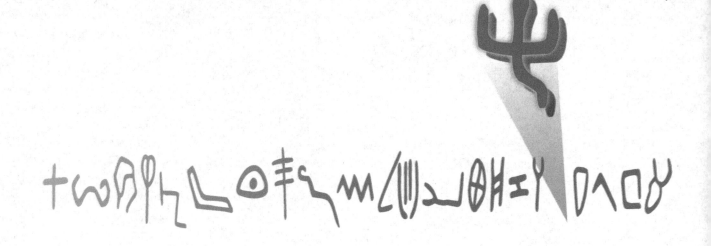

And saw...
a man that said,

24

†ⲱ𝔓𝖍ᒣᒣ⊙𝔽𝔮ⲙ⟨Ⰾ⟩ᴚ⊕Ⴙ⹀Ỵ𝚿ᗰ⋀ᗡ𝖸

Mr. Ox got so scared,
he ran to the other side of the tent.

26

He tripped on a...

28

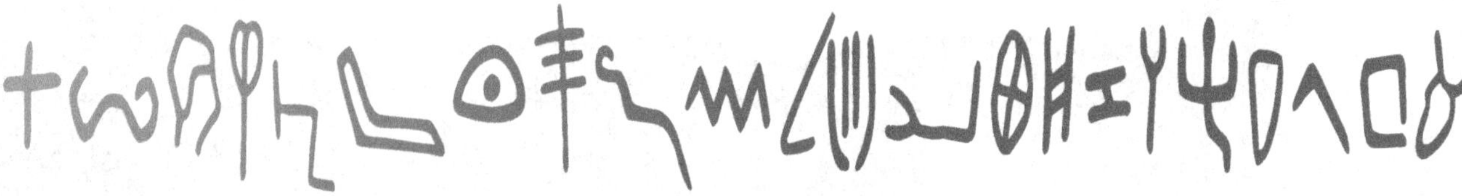

All of a sudden, he saw a garden...

And it had a...

32

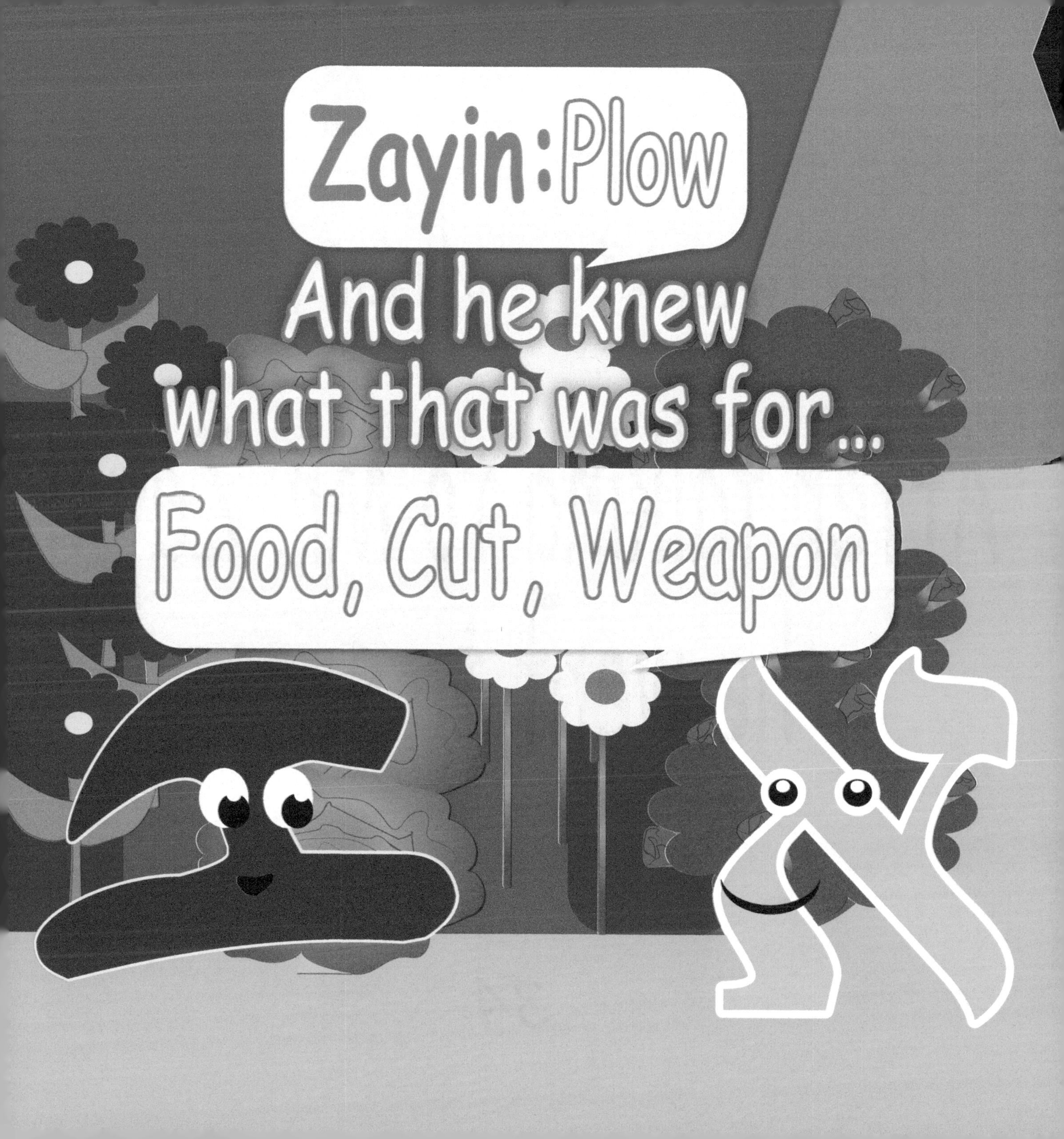
Zayin: Plow
And he knew what that was for...
Food, Cut, Weapon

After talking to Mr. Zayin, he went to see...

34

✝ꙮ🜚ꝑꞀ꜂∟⊙⧧ꙍᷓ﹏⦗⫶⦘⌐⊖⊞⩶Ɏꟓꝺ⌂⋀⌂⅄

"Mr. Ox, there's no way
I'm letting you in this house,"
exclaimed Chet.

Mr. Ox said, "That's ok, I'm just
looking around."

36

So, he went back to the front yard and there in front of the door was...

38

So, Mr. Ox wanted to take the basket back to the backyard, but he needed some help

And then he saw...

†ⲱꙮ𝔊𝔭𝔥ㄴ◒⊙𝔈𝔯𝔪⸜⦗⫯⫯⦘⫝⫝◫⧲Ξ𝖸Ψ𝖥▯ʌ▱𝔶

...Coming down the path.

Mr. Ox said, "Heyyyy, Yodi, Yodi, Yodi, Yodi"

"Can you help me please?"

He said, "Well I think"...

..."could help you better."
So, then
Mr. Ox said, "I'll just use this"...

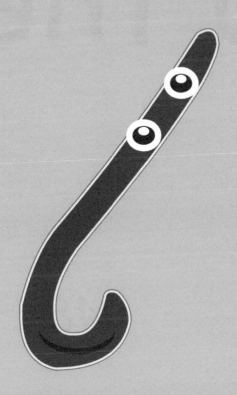

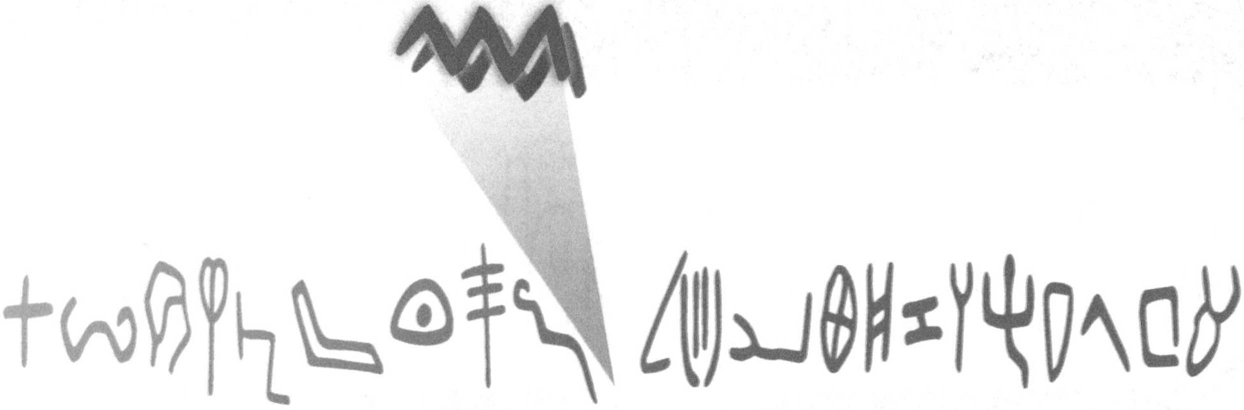

So then...

†ⵥⵀⵖ⵫ⵊⵏⵣ⊙⧧⳥Ⱑ⍦Ⳡⴺⵟⴼⵣⴻⵥ⳥ⵄⵀ⍉⏃ⴾ

...came flowing over
and said,
"Hey, Mr. Ox, what
are you doing?"

50

ᏟᎳᎤᏂᎷᏃᎾᏞᎾᎥ⊙ᕁᏓᒐᏔᏛᏔᏋᏈᏂᎥᏌᏏᏌᎠᏱ

Mr. Ox said, "Well I'm trying to get this Tet over to Mr. Zayin." Then Mem said, "Maybe you should include"...

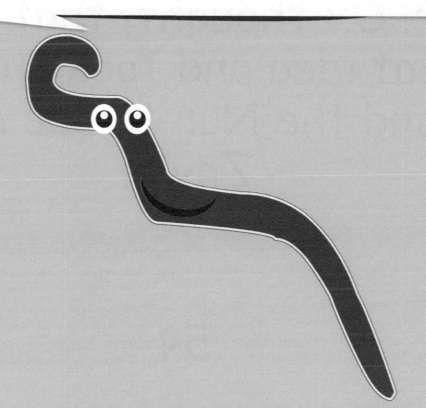

†ᗽᗝᗝᗅᑭᒾ⌐⊙ɀᔕⱮᑓﺍﺍﺍﻟﻟﺍﻟﻟ

...."in your basket!"
Mr. Ox thought, that was a
great idea and took the Tet
and the Nun to see Mr.
Zayin.

Then, Mr. Ox said, "We have to protect this garden."
Mr. Zayin said, "I have just the thing and he called...

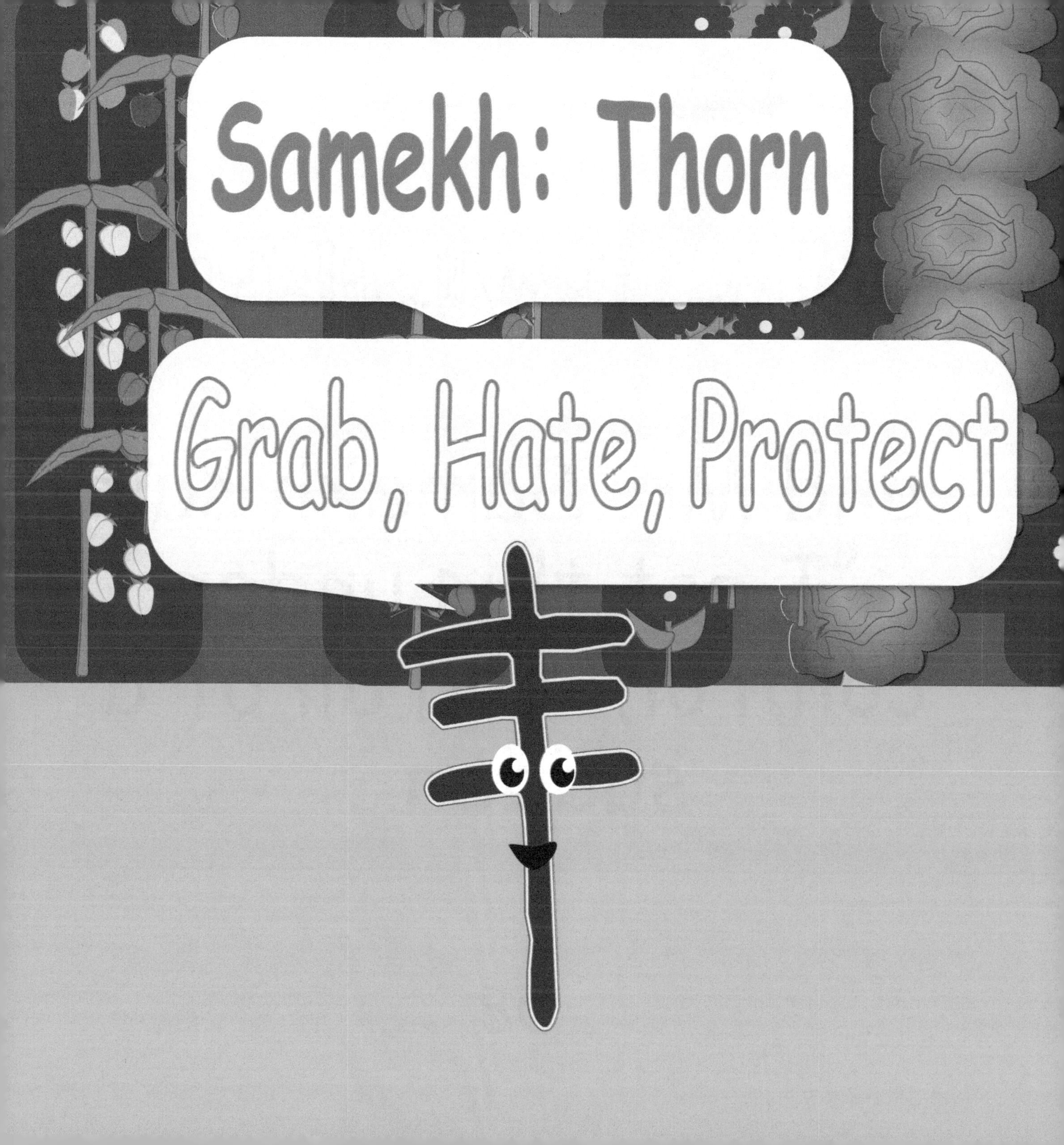
Samekh: Thorn
Grab, Hate, Protect

...and Mr. Samekh said, "I got this under control," and all of a sudden...

58

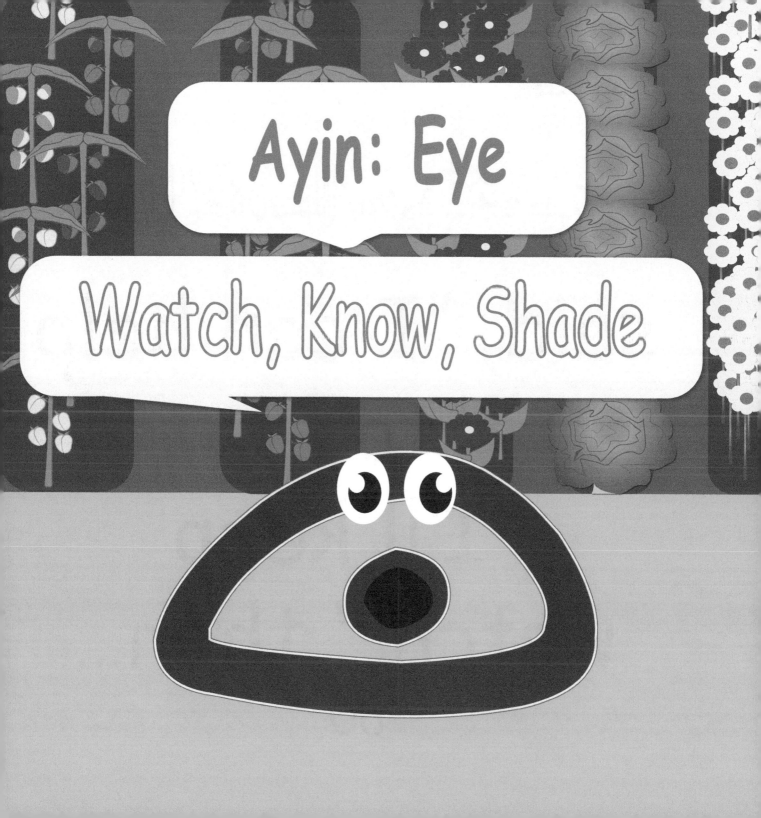

✝ω⏀⑂↾⇃ ⊙⧧⌇ᴟ㎝⟨⫴⟩⏌⊖⊞≡⋎⅄◖∧⬭⍬

said, "I can help too."
"I'll keep watch," then...

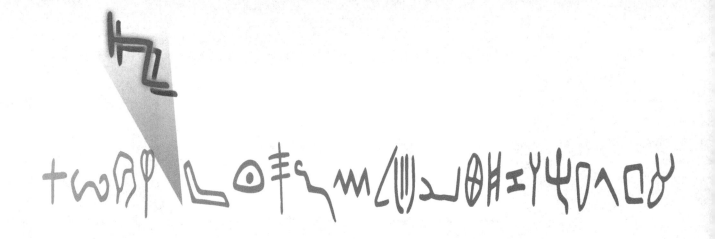

...he said, " I'll
blow anyone away that tries
to come near our Garden."
Mr. Ox was so excited about
everyone wanting to help,
then someone mysterious...

62

✝ᗰ⦾⋔ᒣᒨᗣ◉ᔕᒿᒧᗰ〱Ⴍ⅃ᗒ⊞ᵻᴻᴕᗞᴧᗒᗞᶲ

appeared...

†ᗡ〜B ⼐ᒪ☉ⷪ〜ᗯ⦅⫴⦆⥿⊖Ⴙ⹀Ⴑ⾔Ʊ◻⋀◻

...he was next to the
garden, peeking
around the corner.
But he was nice. So
everyone went to sleep for
the night
and had a fun sleepover!
66

†ᕙⵏᗒᎮᒇ┗◎‡ᕲᥬⵎ⟮Ⱳ┘⊕☩ΞꙌ⨇◊∧ᗐᎧ

In the morning...

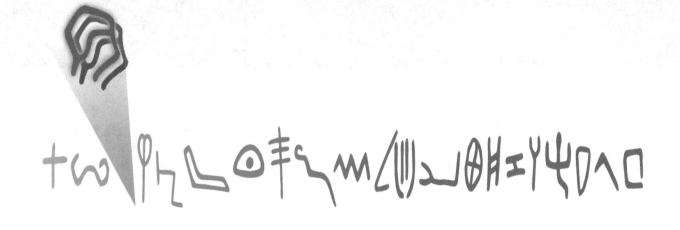

Started to rise and shine on everyone! They all slowly woke up (yawn)...

70

...and started
to clean up.

Then...

⟨symbols⟩

...came over to give everyone breakfast. They were all so excited about the sleepover, and they loooved pancakes and syrup!

74

Then, all of a sudden...

...said, "I can eat all this yummy breakfast all by myself!"

✝〰️𝔊𝔭ꙨꝆ◖⊙ⴲꝰм⟮Ш⟄⊕Ⴙ𐤇ΥΨ🝐ᐱ🝐ᕐ

But wait...

†ᗯ₲ꟼꜱㄥ◎₮ꝭᛘᗰ⟨Ⱳ⟆ⱱ⊖Ⱨ꞊ɎꝮᗡᐱ◻ᎧᎩ

...Jumped in front
of Shin and stopped
him from eating all
the yummy food!

82

All the friends shared
and had a fun day
at the tent and
the Garden.

And that is the amazing origin of meanings behind the Hebrew Alphabet (Aleph Bet :)

The End

BONUS!

Hebrew Charts

Next Two Pages!

87

Ancient Hebrew Chart

Chet	Zayin	Vav	Hey	Dalet	Gimel	Bet	Aleph
Ayin	Samekh	Nun	Mem	Lamed	Kaf	Yod	Tet
		Tav	Shin	Resh	Quf	Tsade	Pey

Modern Hebrew Chart

אבגדהוזחטיכלמנסעפצקרשת

ח Chet	ז Zayin	ו Vav	ה Hey	ד Dalet	ג Gimel	ב Bet	א Aleph
ע Ayin	ס Samekh	נ Nun	מ Mem	ל Lamed	כ Kaf	י Yod	ט Tet
		ת Tav	ש Shin	ר Resh	ק Quf	צ Tsade	פ Pey

Did you enjoy this book?

If so,
leave us a review!
Reviews help us to continue making
awesome books and products for you
And others :)
Oh, and be sure to explore our other
books and shops with all types of
Bible based learning and practical life products!

More Hebrew Learning Books

https://amzn.to/4cdMMYX

Bible Based Etsy Shops

https://shalomshoppes.etsy.com

https://biblelearninglab.etsy.

 **KingdomKhai Website**
https://www.kingdomkhai.com

91

Made in United States
Orlando, FL
19 December 2024

56183568R10057